Homemade Pasta Cookbook

By CARLA HUTSON

Copyright 2024 By CARLA HUTSON. All rights reserved.

No part of this book may be reproduced in any form or by any electronic or mechanical means, including information storage and retrieval systems, without written permission from the author, except for the use of brief quotations in a book review.

Table of Contents

Tips and Techniques for Pasta Dough 6

Brown Rice Pasta Dough 8

Quinoa Pasta Dough 9

Chickpea Pasta Dough 10

Buckwheat Pasta Dough 11

Sweet Potato Pasta Dough 12

Almond Flour Pasta Dough 13

Corn Flour Pasta Dough... 14

Sorghum Flour Pasta Dough 15

Whole Wheat Pasta Dough 16

Spinach Pasta Dough 17

Herb Pasta Dough 18

Lemon Pepper Pasta Dough.. 19

Sun-Dried Tomato Pasta Dough 20

Pumpkin Pasta Dough.. 21

Garlic and Herb Pasta Dough 22

Mushroom Pasta Dough.. 24

Turmeric and Ginger Pasta Dough 25

Matcha Pasta Dough 26

Pesto Pasta Dough.. 27

Charred Corn Pasta Dough 28

Roasted Red Pepper Pasta Dough.. 30

Lemon and Herb Pasta Dough 32

Chia Seed Pasta Dough 33

Charcoal Pasta Dough.. 34

Tomato Pasta Dough.. 35

Turmeric Pasta Dough 36

Beet Pasta Dough 37

Squid Ink Pasta Dough 38

Chili Pepper Pasta Dough 39

Saffron Pasta Dough 40

Porcini Mushroom Pasta Dough 42

Carrot Pasta Dough 43

Hibiscus Pasta Dough 44

Beetroot Pasta Dough 45

Coconut Pasta Dough 46

Lavender Pasta Dough 47

Butternut Squash Pasta Dough 48

Ginger Turmeric Pasta Dough 49

Lemon Basil Pasta Dough 50

Whole Wheat Lasagna Dough 51

Spinach Lasagna Dough 52

Herb Lasagna Dough 53

Almond Flour Lasagna Dough 54

Brown Rice Lasagna Dough 55

Quinoa Flour Lasagna Dough 56

Tapioca Flour Lasagna Dough 57

Pasta Sause 58

Classic Marinara Sauce 59

Creamy Alfredo Sauce 60

Spicy Arrabbiata Sauce 61

Pesto Sauce 62

Roasted Red Pepper Sauce 63

Lemon Garlic Butter Sauce 65

Mushroom Cream Sauce 66

Spinach and Tomato Sauce	67
Roasted Vegetable Sauce	68
Garlic Mushroom Marinara Sauce	70
Lemon Ricotta Pasta Sauce	71
Coconut Curry Pasta Sauce	72
Sun-Dried Tomato Pesto Pasta Sauce	74
Ginger Miso Pasta Sauce	75
Creamy Walnut Sage Pasta Sauce	77
Thai Peanut Sauce	79
Thai Basil Pesto	81
Thai Green Curry Sauce	82
Thai Sweet Chili Sauce	83
Vegetarian Carbonara Sauce	85

Tips and Techniques for Pasta Dough

Pasta dough is the fundamental mixture of flour, eggs, and sometimes water or oil, used as the base for making pasta from scratch. It serves as the foundation for various types of pasta, including spaghetti, fettuccine, ravioli, and more. The ingredients are combined, kneaded, and rolled out to form thin sheets or shapes, which are then cooked in boiling water to create the final pasta dish. Homemade pasta dough offers a fresh, tender texture and allows for endless customization with different flours, flavorings, and shapes.

- Use the Right Flour: The best flour for pasta dough is typically "00" flour, which is finely ground and has a high protein content. However, you can also use all-purpose flour if you can't find "00" flour.
- Weigh Ingredients: Pasta dough is sensitive to proportions, so it's best to weigh your ingredients rather than relying on volume measurements for accuracy.
- Eggs: While traditional pasta dough uses whole eggs, some recipes call for just egg yolks or a combination of whole eggs and egg yolks. Using just egg yolks will yield a richer dough, while whole eggs provide structure.
- Mixing: Start by making a well with the flour on a clean surface. Gradually incorporate the eggs into the flour, using a fork or your fingers to mix. Be patient and mix the ingredients until a shaggy dough forms.
- Kneading: Once the dough comes together, knead it for about 8-10 minutes until it becomes smooth and elastic. This helps develop the gluten, giving the pasta its characteristic texture.
- Resting: After kneading, wrap the dough in plastic wrap and let it rest at room temperature for at least 30 minutes. This allows the gluten to relax, making the dough easier to roll out.
- Rolling: Use a pasta machine or a rolling pin to roll out the dough to your desired thickness. Start with the widest setting and gradually decrease the thickness until you reach your desired thickness.

- Flouring: While rolling out the dough, make sure to flour it lightly as needed to prevent sticking. Too much flour can make the dough dry and tough, so use it sparingly.
- Shaping: Once the dough is rolled out, you can shape it into various pasta shapes such as fettuccine, spaghetti, or ravioli. Make sure to flour the pasta sheets or shapes lightly to prevent them from sticking together.
- Cooking: Fresh pasta cooks much faster than dried pasta, usually in just 2-4 minutes depending on the thickness. Make sure to salt the boiling water generously before adding the pasta, and stir gently to prevent sticking.
- Testing for Doneness: The best way to test if fresh pasta is cooked is to taste it. It should be tender but still have a slight bite (al dente).
- Save Some Pasta Water: Before draining the pasta, reserve some of the cooking water. This starchy water can be used to thin out pasta sauces and help them adhere better to the pasta.

Brown Rice Pasta Dough

Brown rice pasta dough offers a nutritious and gluten-free alternative to traditional pasta. This dough is made with brown rice flour and has a slightly nutty flavor and a hearty texture. It pairs well with various sauces and toppings, making it a versatile option for any meal.

Total Time Cooking: Approximately 1 hour

Ingredients:

- 2 cups brown rice flour
- 3 large eggs
- 1/2 teaspoon salt

Directions:

1. In a mixing bowl, combine brown rice flour and salt.
2. Make a well in the center and add the eggs.
3. Gradually incorporate the flour into the eggs until a dough forms.
4. Knead the dough for 5-10 minutes until smooth and elastic.
5. If the dough is too dry, add a little water, one tablespoon at a time, until the desired consistency is reached.
6. Wrap the dough in plastic wrap and let it rest for at least 30 minutes.
7. Roll out the dough to your desired thickness and cut it into desired shapes using a pasta machine or hand.
8. Cook the pasta in boiling salted water for 2-3 minutes or until al dente. Serve with your favorite sauce and toppings.

Quinoa Pasta Dough

Quinoa pasta dough is a protein-rich and gluten-free option for pasta lovers. Made with quinoa flour, this dough has a delicate flavor and a light texture. It pairs well with creamy and tomato-based sauces, making it a versatile choice for any occasion.

Total Time Cooking: Approximately 1 hour

Ingredients:

- 2 cups quinoa flour
- 3 large eggs
- 1/2 teaspoon salt

Directions:

1. In a mixing bowl, combine quinoa flour and salt.
2. Make a well in the center and add the eggs.
3. Gradually incorporate the flour into the eggs until a dough forms.
4. Knead the dough for 5-10 minutes until smooth and elastic.
5. If the dough is too dry, add a little water, one tablespoon at a time, until the desired consistency is reached.
6. Wrap the dough in plastic wrap and let it rest for at least 30 minutes.
7. Roll out the dough to your desired thickness and cut it into desired shapes using a pasta machine or hand.
8. Cook the pasta in boiling salted water for 2-3 minutes or until al dente. Serve with your favorite sauce and toppings.

Chickpea Pasta Dough

Chickpea pasta dough offers a hearty and flavorful option for gluten-free pasta. Made with chickpea flour, this dough has a nutty taste and a satisfying texture. It pairs well with bold and spicy sauces and creamy and herbaceous ones, making it a versatile choice for any palate.

Total Time Cooking: Approximately 1 hour

Ingredients:

- 2 cups chickpea flour
- 3 large eggs
- 1/2 teaspoon salt

Directions:

1. In a mixing bowl, combine chickpea flour and salt.
2. Make a well in the center and add the eggs.
3. Gradually incorporate the flour into the eggs until a dough forms.
4. Knead the dough for 5-10 minutes until smooth and elastic.
5. If the dough is too dry, add a little water, one tablespoon at a time, until the desired consistency is reached.
6. Wrap the dough in plastic wrap and let it rest for at least 30 minutes.
7. Roll out the dough to your desired thickness and cut it into desired shapes using a pasta machine or hand.
8. Cook the pasta in boiling salted water for 2-3 minutes or until al dente. Serve with your favorite sauce and toppings.

Buckwheat Pasta Dough

Buckwheat pasta dough offers a nutty and robust flavor to your gluten-free pasta. Made with buckwheat flour, this dough has a rich taste and a slightly chewy texture. It pairs well with earthy and savory sauces and creamy and cheese-based ones, making it a versatile option for any meal.

Total Time Cooking: Approximately 1 hour

Ingredients:

- 2 cups buckwheat flour
- 3 large eggs
- 1/2 teaspoon salt

Directions:

1. In a mixing bowl, combine buckwheat flour and salt.
2. Make a well in the center and add the eggs.
3. Gradually incorporate the flour into the eggs until a dough forms.
4. Knead the dough for 5-10 minutes until smooth and elastic.
5. If the dough is too dry, add a little water, one tablespoon at a time, until the desired consistency is reached.
6. Wrap the dough in plastic wrap and let it rest for at least 30 minutes.
7. Roll out the dough to your desired thickness and cut it into desired shapes using a pasta machine or hand.
8. Cook the pasta in boiling salted water for 2-3 minutes or until al dente. Serve with your favorite sauce and toppings.

Sweet Potato Pasta Dough

Sweet Potato Pasta Dough adds a touch of sweetness and vibrant color to your gluten-free pasta. This dough is made with mashed sweet potatoes and offers a unique flavor profile and soft texture. Pair it with a creamy garlic sauce or savory sage brown butter for a comforting and delicious dish.

Total Time Cooking: Approximately 1 hour

Ingredients:

- 2 cups gluten-free all-purpose flour
- 1 cup mashed sweet potatoes (cooked and cooled)
- 2 large eggs
- 1/2 teaspoon salt

Directions:

1. In a mixing bowl, combine gluten-free all-purpose flour and salt.

2. Add mashed sweet potatoes and eggs to the flour mixture.

3. Mix until a dough forms, adding more flour if necessary to achieve consistency.

4. Knead the dough for 5-10 minutes until smooth and elastic.

5. Wrap the dough in plastic wrap and let it rest for at least 30 minutes.

6. Roll out the dough to your desired thickness and cut it into desired shapes using a pasta machine or hand.

7. Cook the pasta in boiling salted water for 2-3 minutes or until al dente. Serve with your favorite sauce and toppings.

Almond Flour Pasta Dough

Almond Flour Pasta Dough offers a nutty flavor and a delicate texture to your gluten-free pasta. Made with almond flour, this dough is rich in protein and adds a subtle sweetness to your dishes. Pair it with a creamy Alfredo sauce or a fresh tomato and basil sauce for a flavorful meal.

Total Time Cooking: Approximately 1 hour

Ingredients:

- 2 cups almond flour
- 2 large eggs
- 1/2 teaspoon salt

Directions:

1. In a mixing bowl, combine almond flour and salt.
2. Make a well in the center and add the eggs.
3. Gradually incorporate the flour into the eggs until a dough forms.
4. Knead the dough for 5-10 minutes until smooth and elastic.
5. If the dough is too dry, add a little water, one tablespoon at a time, until the desired consistency is reached.
6. Wrap the dough in plastic wrap and let it rest for at least 30 minutes.
7. Roll out the dough to your desired thickness and cut it into desired shapes using a pasta machine or hand.
8. Cook the pasta in boiling salted water for 2-3 minutes or until al dente. Serve with your favorite sauce and toppings.

Corn Flour Pasta Dough

Corn Flour Pasta Dough offers your gluten-free pasta a slightly sweet and earthy flavor. This dough is made with corn flour, has a tender texture, and pairs well with various sauces. For a delicious meal, try it with a rich mushroom cream sauce or a simple garlic and olive oil dressing.

Total Time Cooking: Approximately 1 hour

Ingredients:

- 2 cups corn flour (also known as masa harina)
- 2 large eggs
- 1/2 teaspoon salt

Directions:

1. In a mixing bowl, combine corn flour and salt.

2. Make a well in the center and add the eggs.

3. Gradually incorporate the flour into the eggs until a dough forms.

4. Knead the dough for 5-10 minutes until smooth and elastic.

5. If the dough is too dry, add a little water, one tablespoon at a time, until the desired consistency is reached.

6. Wrap the dough in plastic wrap and let it rest for at least 30 minutes.

7. Roll out the dough to your desired thickness and cut it into desired shapes using a pasta machine or hand.

8. Cook the pasta in boiling salted water for 2-3 minutes or until al dente. Serve with your favorite sauce and toppings.

Sorghum Flour Pasta Dough

Sorghum Flour Pasta Dough offers a mild and slightly sweet flavor to your gluten-free pasta. This dough is made with sorghum flour, has a tender texture, and pairs well with various sauces. For a flavorful meal, try it with a spicy arrabbiata sauce or creamy pesto.

Total Time Cooking: Approximately 1 hour

Ingredients:

- 2 cups sorghum flour
- 2 large eggs
- 1/2 teaspoon salt

Directions:

1. In a mixing bowl, combine sorghum flour and salt.
2. Make a well in the center and add the eggs.
3. Gradually incorporate the flour into the eggs until a dough forms.
4. Knead the dough for 5-10 minutes until smooth and elastic.
5. If the dough is too dry, add a little water, one tablespoon at a time, until the desired consistency is reached.
6. Wrap the dough in plastic wrap and let it rest for at least 30 minutes.
7. Roll out the dough to your desired thickness and cut it into desired shapes using a pasta machine or hand.
8. Cook the pasta in boiling salted water for 2-3 minutes or until al dente. Serve with your favorite sauce and toppings.

Whole Wheat Pasta Dough

This Whole Wheat Pasta Dough recipe is a healthier alternative to traditional pasta dough, using whole wheat flour for added fiber and nutrients. It's easy to make and has a nutty flavor that pairs well with various sauces and toppings. Plus, it's a great way to incorporate more whole grains into your diet.

Total Time Cooking: Approximately 30 minutes

Ingredients:

- 1 1/2 cups whole wheat flour
- 1/2 cup all-purpose flour
- 2 large eggs
- 1/2 teaspoon salt
- Water, as needed

Directions:

1. In a large mixing bowl, combine whole wheat flour, all-purpose flour, and salt.

2. Make a well in the center and crack the eggs.

3. Gradually incorporate the flour into the eggs until a dough forms, adding water as needed to achieve consistency.

4. Knead the dough for 5-10 minutes until smooth and elastic.

5. Wrap the dough in plastic wrap and let it rest for at least 30 minutes.

6. Roll out the dough to the desired thickness and cut it into desired shapes using a pasta machine or hand.

7. Cook the pasta in boiling salted water for 2-3 minutes or until al dente. Serve with your favorite sauce and toppings.

Spinach Pasta Dough

This Spinach Pasta Dough recipe adds a vibrant green color and subtle earthy flavor to your homemade pasta. Made with pureed spinach, this dough is visually appealing and packed with nutrients. It's fun to sneak in some greens and impress your guests with your culinary skills.

Total Time Cooking: Approximately 30 minutes

Ingredients:

- 2 cups all-purpose flour
- 1/2 cup pureed spinach (cooked and squeezed dry)
- 2 large eggs
- 1/2 teaspoon salt

Directions:

1. In a mixing bowl, combine all-purpose flour and salt.

2. Make a well in the center and add pureed spinach and eggs.

3. Gradually incorporate the flour into the wet ingredients until a dough forms.

4. Knead the dough for 5-10 minutes until smooth and elastic.

5. Wrap the dough in plastic wrap and let it rest for at least 30 minutes.

6. Roll out the dough to the desired thickness and cut it into desired shapes using a pasta machine or hand.

7. Cook the pasta in boiling salted water for 2-3 minutes or until al dente. Serve with your favorite sauce and toppings.

Herb Pasta Dough

This Herb Pasta Dough recipe is infused with the flavors of fresh herbs, adding a burst of freshness to your homemade pasta. Use a combination of your favorite herbs, such as basil, parsley, or thyme, to customize the flavor to your liking. It's a simple yet elegant way to elevate your pasta dishes.

Total Time Cooking: Approximately 30 minutes

Ingredients:

- 2 cups all-purpose flour
- 2 tablespoons fresh herbs, finely chopped (such as basil, parsley, or thyme)
- 2 large eggs
- 1/2 teaspoon salt

Directions:

1. combine all-purpose flour, chopped herbs, and salt in a mixing bowl.
2. Make a well in the center and crack the eggs.
3. Gradually incorporate the flour into the eggs until a dough forms.
4. Knead the dough for 5-10 minutes until smooth and elastic.
5. Wrap the dough in plastic wrap and let it rest for at least 30 minutes.
6. Roll out the dough to the desired thickness and cut it into desired shapes using a pasta machine or hand.
7. Cook the pasta in boiling salted water for 2-3 minutes or until al dente. Serve with your favorite sauce and toppings.

Lemon Pepper Pasta Dough

Lemon Pepper Pasta Dough adds a refreshing citrusy flavor and subtle heat to your homemade pasta. Made with lemon zest and freshly cracked black pepper, this dough is bright and zesty, perfect for pairing with light sauces and seafood dishes. It's a delightful twist on traditional pasta that will tantalize your taste buds.

Total Time Cooking: Approximately 30 minutes

Ingredients:

- 2 cups all-purpose flour
- Zest of 2 lemons
- 2 teaspoons freshly cracked black pepper
- 2 large eggs
- 1/2 teaspoon salt

Directions:

1. combine all-purpose flour, lemon zest, black pepper, and salt in a mixing bowl.

2. Make a well in the center and crack the eggs.

3. Gradually incorporate the flour into the eggs until a dough forms.

4. Knead the dough for 5-10 minutes until smooth and elastic.

5. Wrap the dough in plastic wrap and let it rest for at least 30 minutes.

6. Roll out the dough to the desired thickness and cut it into desired shapes using a pasta machine or hand.

7. Cook the pasta in boiling salted water for 2-3 minutes or until al dente. Serve with your favorite sauce and toppings.

Sun-Dried Tomato Pasta Dough

Sun-dried tomato Pasta Dough adds a rich, umami flavor and vibrant color to your homemade pasta. Made with pureed sun-dried tomatoes, this dough is savory and aromatic, perfect for pairing with creamy sauces or hearty vegetable dishes. It's a delightful departure from traditional pasta that will tantalize your taste buds.

Total Time Cooking: Approximately 1 hour

Ingredients:

- 1/2 cup sun-dried tomatoes (packed in oil), drained
- 2 cups all-purpose flour
- 2 large eggs
- 1/2 teaspoon salt

Directions:

1. In a food processor, puree sun-dried tomatoes until smooth.

2. combine sun-dried tomato puree, all-purpose flour, and salt in a mixing bowl.

3. Make a well in the center and crack the eggs.

4. Gradually incorporate the flour into the eggs until a dough forms.

5. Knead the dough for 5-10 minutes until smooth and elastic.

6. Wrap the dough in plastic wrap and let it rest for at least 30 minutes.

7. Roll out the dough to the desired thickness and cut it into desired shapes using a pasta machine or by hand.

8. Cook the pasta in boiling salted water for 2-3 minutes or until al dente. Serve with your favorite sauce and toppings.

Pumpkin Pasta Dough

Pumpkin Pasta Dough adds a subtle sweetness and vibrant orange color to your homemade pasta. This dough is rich and flavorful and made with pumpkin puree, perfect for pairing with creamy sauces or savory toppings. It's a festive twist on traditional pasta that will delight your senses and warm your soul.

Total Time Cooking: Approximately 1 hour

Ingredients:

- 1/2 cup pumpkin puree
- 2 cups all-purpose flour
- 2 large eggs
- 1/2 teaspoon salt
- Pinch of nutmeg (optional)

Directions:

1. In a mixing bowl, combine pumpkin puree, all-purpose flour, salt, and nutmeg (if using).

2. Make a well in the center and crack the eggs.

3. Gradually incorporate the flour into the eggs until a dough forms.

4. Knead the dough for 5-10 minutes until smooth and elastic.

5. Wrap the dough in plastic wrap and let it rest for at least 30 minutes.

6. Roll out the dough to the desired thickness and cut it into desired shapes using a pasta machine or hand.

7. Cook the pasta in boiling salted water for 2-3 minutes or until al dente. Serve with your favorite sauce and toppings.

Garlic and Herb Pasta Dough

Garlic and Herb Pasta Dough adds a flavorful punch to your homemade pasta. This dough is aromatic and savory and is infused with minced garlic, fresh herbs like rosemary and thyme, and a hint of black pepper. It pairs well with various sauces, from simple olive oil and garlic to creamy Alfredo.

Total Time Cooking: Approximately 1 hour

Ingredients:

- 2 cups all-purpose flour
- 2 large eggs
- 2 cloves garlic, minced
- 1 tablespoon fresh rosemary, finely chopped
- 1 tablespoon fresh thyme leaves, finely chopped
- 1/2 teaspoon black pepper
- 1/2 teaspoon salt

Directions:

1. Mix all-purpose flour, minced garlic, chopped rosemary, chopped thyme, black pepper, and salt in a mixing bowl.

2. Make a well in the center and crack the eggs.

3. Gradually incorporate the flour into the eggs until a dough forms.

4. Knead the dough for 5-10 minutes until smooth and elastic.

5. Wrap the dough in plastic wrap and let it rest for at 30 minutes.

6. Roll out the dough to the desired thickness and cut it into desired shapes using a pasta machine or hand.

7.   Cook the pasta in boiling salted water for 2-3 minutes or until al dente. Serve with your favorite sauce and toppings.

Mushroom Pasta Dough

Mushroom Pasta Dough adds a rich and earthy flavor to your homemade pasta. Made with dried porcini mushrooms that have been rehydrated and finely chopped, this dough has a unique depth of flavor that pairs well with creamy sauces or hearty ragùs. It's a delicious way to incorporate mushrooms into your pasta dishes.

Total Time Cooking: Approximately 1 hour

Ingredients:

- 1/2 cup dried porcini mushrooms
- 2 cups all-purpose flour
- 2 large eggs
- 1/2 teaspoon salt

Directions:

1. rehydrate dried porcini mushrooms in warm water in a small bowl for 20-30 minutes. Drain and finely chop.

2. combine all-purpose flour, chopped porcini mushrooms, and salt in a mixing bowl.

3. Make a well in the center and crack the eggs.

4. Gradually incorporate the flour into the eggs until a dough forms.

5. Knead the dough for 5-10 minutes until smooth and elastic.

6. Wrap the dough in plastic wrap and let it rest for at least 30 minutes.

7. Roll out the dough to the desired thickness and cut it into desired shapes using a pasta machine or hand.

8. Cook the pasta in boiling salted water for 2-3 minutes or until al dente. Serve with your favorite sauce and toppings.

Turmeric and Ginger Pasta Dough

Turmeric and Ginger Pasta Dough add warmth and spice to your homemade pasta. Infused with ground turmeric and fresh ginger, this dough has a vibrant golden color and a subtle heat that pairs well with aromatic Asian-inspired sauces or creamy coconut curry. It's a flavorful twist on traditional pasta that will awaken your taste buds.

Total Time Cooking: Approximately 1 hour

Ingredients:

- 2 cups all-purpose flour
- 2 teaspoons ground turmeric
- 1 tablespoon fresh ginger, grated
- 2 large eggs
- 1/2 teaspoon salt

Directions:

1. combine all-purpose flour, ground turmeric, grated ginger, and salt in a mixing bowl.
2. Make a well in the center and crack the eggs.
3. Gradually incorporate the flour into the eggs until a dough forms.
4. Knead the dough for 5-10 minutes until smooth and elastic.
5. Wrap the dough in plastic wrap and let it rest for at least 30 minutes.
6. Roll out the dough to the desired thickness and cut it into desired shapes using a pasta machine or hand.
7. Cook the pasta in boiling salted water for 2-3 minutes or until al dente. Serve with your favorite sauce and toppings.

Matcha Pasta Dough

Matcha Pasta Dough adds a vibrant green color and subtle earthy flavor to your homemade pasta. Made with high-quality matcha powder, this dough is antioxidant-rich and has a unique taste that pairs well with savory or sweet sauces. It's a fun and flavorful way to incorporate matcha into your pasta dishes.

Total Time Cooking: Approximately 1 hour

Ingredients:

- 2 cups all-purpose flour
- 2 tablespoons high-quality matcha powder
- 2 large eggs
- 1/2 teaspoon salt

Directions:

1. combine all-purpose flour, matcha powder, and salt in a mixing bowl.
2. Make a well in the center and crack the eggs.
3. Gradually incorporate the flour into the eggs until a dough forms.
4. Knead the dough for 5-10 minutes until smooth and elastic.
5. Wrap the dough in plastic wrap and let it rest for at least 30 minutes.
6. Roll out the dough to the desired thickness and cut it into desired shapes using a pasta machine or hand.
7. Cook the pasta in boiling salted water for 2-3 minutes or until al dente. Serve with your favorite sauce and toppings.

Pesto Pasta Dough

Pesto Pasta Dough infuses your homemade pasta with the vibrant basil, garlic, pine nuts, and Parmesan cheese flavors. This dough offers a delightful twist on traditional pasta, providing freshness and herbaceousness in every bite. Pair it with olive oil and garlic sauce, or toss it with cherry tomatoes and fresh mozzarella for a delightful summer dish.

Total Time Cooking: Approximately 1 hour

Ingredients:

- 2 cups all-purpose flour
- 2 tablespoons store-bought or homemade pesto
- 2 large eggs
- 1/2 teaspoon salt

Directions:

1. combine all-purpose flour, pesto, and salt in a mixing bowl.
2. Make a well in the center and crack the eggs.
3. Gradually incorporate the flour into the eggs until a dough forms.
4. Knead the dough for 5-10 minutes until smooth and elastic.
5. Wrap the dough in plastic wrap and let it rest for at least 30 minutes.
6. Roll out the dough to the desired thickness and cut it into desired shapes using a pasta machine or hand.
7. Cook the pasta in boiling salted water for 2-3 minutes or until al dente. Serve with your favorite sauce and toppings.

Charred Corn Pasta Dough

Charred Corn Pasta Dough incorporates the smoky sweetness of charred corn into your homemade pasta, resulting in a unique and flavorful dish. The corn kernels are grilled until lightly charred, then blended into the pasta dough with a hint of chili flakes for a touch of heat. Serve this pasta with a creamy sauce or a light vinaigrette for a delightful summer meal.

Total Time Cooking: Approximately 1 hour

Ingredients:

- 2 cups all-purpose flour
- 1/2 cup grilled corn kernels, charred and cooled
- 2 large eggs
- 1/2 teaspoon chili flakes (optional)
- 1/2 teaspoon salt

Directions:

1. In a food processor, pulse grilled corn kernels until coarsely chopped.
2. In a mixing bowl, combine all-purpose flour, chopped corn kernels, chili flakes (if using), and salt.
3. Make a well in the center and crack the eggs.
4. Gradually incorporate the flour into the eggs until a dough forms.
5. Knead the dough for 5-10 minutes until smooth and elastic.
6. Wrap the dough in plastic wrap and let it rest for at least 30 minutes.
7. Roll out the dough to the desired thickness and cut it into desired shapes using a pasta machine or by hand.

8. Cook the pasta in boiling salted water for 2-3 minutes or until al dente. Serve with your favorite sauce and toppings.

Roasted Red Pepper Pasta Dough

Roasted Red Pepper Pasta Dough infuses your homemade pasta with roasted red peppers' sweet and smoky flavor. The peppers are charred until tender, then pureed and mixed into the pasta dough, along with a touch of garlic and paprika for added depth of flavor. Serve this pasta with a creamy Alfredo sauce or a simple tomato basil sauce for a delightful meal.

Total Time Cooking: Approximately 1 hour

Ingredients:

- 2 cups all-purpose flour
- 1/2 cup roasted red peppers, drained and pureed
- 2 cloves garlic, minced
- 1/2 teaspoon smoked paprika
- 2 large eggs
- 1/2 teaspoon salt

Directions:

1. In a food processor, pure roasted red peppers until smooth.

2. combine all-purpose flour, red pepper puree, minced garlic, smoked paprika, and salt in a mixing bowl.

3. Make a well in the center and crack the eggs.

4. Gradually incorporate the flour into the eggs until a dough forms.

5. Knead the dough for 5-10 minutes until smooth and elastic.

6. Wrap the dough in plastic wrap and let it rest for at least 30 minutes.

7. Roll out the dough to the desired thickness and cut it into desired shapes using a pasta machine or by hand.

8. Cook the pasta in boiling salted water for 2-3 minutes or until al dente. Serve with your favorite sauce and toppings.

Lemon and Herb Pasta Dough

Lemon and Herb Pasta Dough adds a refreshing citrusy flavor and aromatic herbs to your homemade pasta. Fresh lemon zest, parsley, and basil are mixed into the dough, creating a bright and flavorful dish perfect for spring or summer. Serve this pasta with a light lemon butter sauce or a creamy goat cheese sauce for a delightful meal.

Total Time Cooking: Approximately 1 hour

Ingredients:

- 2 cups all-purpose flour
- Zest of 2 lemons
- 2 tablespoons fresh parsley, finely chopped
- 2 tablespoons fresh basil, finely chopped
- 2 large eggs
- 1/2 teaspoon salt

Directions:

1. combine all-purpose flour, lemon zest, chopped parsley, basil, and salt in a mixing bowl.
2. Make a well in the center and crack the eggs.
3. Gradually incorporate the flour into the eggs until a dough forms.
4. Knead the dough for 5-10 minutes until smooth and elastic.
5. Wrap the dough in plastic wrap and let it rest for at least 30 minutes.
6. Roll out the dough to the desired thickness and cut it into desired shapes using a pasta machine or hand.
7. Cook the pasta in boiling salted water for 2-3 minutes or until al dente. Serve with your favorite sauce and toppings.

Chia Seed Pasta Dough

Chia Seed Pasta Dough adds a nutritional boost to your homemade pasta with chia seeds. These tiny seeds are packed with fiber, protein, and omega-3 fatty acids, making them a nutritious addition to any meal. Mixed into the pasta dough, they add a subtle crunch and a nutty flavor that pairs well with various sauces and toppings. Serve this pasta with a simple olive oil and garlic sauce or a hearty vegetable ragù for a wholesome meal.

Total Time Cooking: Approximately 1 hour

Ingredients:

- 2 cups all-purpose flour
- 2 tablespoons chia seeds
- 2 large eggs
- 1/2 teaspoon salt

Directions:

1. combine all-purpose flour, chia seeds, and salt in a mixing bowl.
2. Make a well in the center and crack the eggs.
3. Gradually incorporate the flour into the eggs until a dough forms.
4. Knead the dough for 5-10 minutes until smooth and elastic.
5. Wrap the dough in plastic wrap and let it rest for at least 30 minutes.
6. Roll out the dough to the desired thickness and cut it into desired shapes using a pasta machine or hand.
7. Cook the pasta in boiling salted water for 2-3 minutes or until al dente. Serve with your favorite sauce and toppings.

Charcoal Pasta Dough

Charcoal Pasta Dough adds a dramatic black color and a unique smoky flavor to your homemade pasta. Activated charcoal powder is mixed into the dough, creating a striking appearance that will impress your dinner guests. This pasta pairs well with creamy sauces or seafood dishes, offering a visually stunning and delicious culinary experience.

Total Time Cooking: Approximately 1 hour

Ingredients:

- 2 cups all-purpose flour
- 1 tablespoon activated charcoal powder
- 2 large eggs
- 1/2 teaspoon salt

Directions:

1. combine all-purpose flour, activated charcoal powder, and salt in a mixing bowl.

2. Make a well in the center and add the eggs.

3. Gradually incorporate the flour into the eggs until a dough forms.

4. Knead the dough for 5-10 minutes until smooth and elastic.

5. Wrap the dough in plastic wrap and let it rest for at least 30 minutes.

6. Roll out the dough to your desired thickness and cut it into desired shapes using a pasta machine or hand.

7. Cook the pasta in boiling salted water for 2-3 minutes or until al dente. Serve with your favorite sauce and toppings.

Tomato Pasta Dough

Tomato Pasta Dough adds a rich tomato flavor and a beautiful red color to your homemade pasta. Made with tomato paste or pureed sun-dried tomatoes, this dough is bursting with savory goodness. It's perfect for pairing with meaty sauces or roasted vegetables, offering a delicious twist on traditional pasta dishes.

Total Time Cooking: Approximately 1 hour

Ingredients:

- 2 cups all-purpose flour
- 1/4 cup tomato paste or pureed sun-dried tomatoes
- 2 large eggs
- 1/2 teaspoon salt

Directions:

1. combine all-purpose flour, tomato paste, pureed sun-dried tomatoes, and salt in a mixing bowl.

2. Make a well in the center and add the eggs.

3. Gradually incorporate the flour into the eggs until a dough forms.

4. Knead the dough for 5-10 minutes until smooth and elastic.

5. Wrap the dough in plastic wrap and let it rest for at least 30 minutes.

6. Roll out the dough to your desired thickness and cut it into desired shapes using a pasta machine or hand.

7. Cook the pasta in boiling salted water for 2-3 minutes or until al dente. Serve with your favorite sauce and toppings.

Turmeric Pasta Dough

Turmeric Pasta Dough adds a vibrant yellow color and a warm, slightly spicy flavor to your homemade pasta. Made with ground turmeric, this dough not only looks beautiful but also offers health benefits thanks to the anti-inflammatory properties of turmeric. Pair it with a creamy coconut curry sauce or a simple garlic and herb dressing for a delicious and nutritious meal.

Total Time Cooking: Approximately 1 hour

Ingredients:

- 2 cups all-purpose flour
- 1 tablespoon ground turmeric
- 2 large eggs
- 1/2 teaspoon salt

Directions:

1. combine all-purpose flour, ground turmeric, and salt in a mixing bowl.
2. Make a well in the center and add the eggs.
3. Gradually incorporate the flour into the eggs until a dough forms.
4. Knead the dough for 5-10 minutes until smooth and elastic.
5. Wrap the dough in plastic wrap and let it rest for at least 30 minutes.
6. Roll out the dough to your desired thickness and cut it into desired shapes using a pasta machine or hand.
7. Cook the pasta in boiling salted water for 2-3 minutes or until al dente. Serve with your favorite sauce and toppings.

Beet Pasta Dough

Beet Pasta Dough adds a vibrant pink color and a subtle earthy sweetness to your homemade pasta. Made with pureed roasted beets, this dough is as nutritious as beautiful. It's perfect for adding a pop of color to your pasta dishes and impressing your guests with culinary creativity. Pair it with a creamy goat cheese sauce or a simple lemon and olive oil dressing for a delightful meal.

Total Time Cooking: Approximately 1 hour

Ingredients:

- 2 cups all-purpose flour
- 1/2 cup roasted beet puree
- 2 large eggs
- 1/2 teaspoon salt

Directions:

1. combine all-purpose flour, roasted beet puree, and salt in a mixing bowl.
2. Make a well in the center and add the eggs.
3. Gradually incorporate the flour into the eggs until a dough forms.
4. Knead the dough for 5-10 minutes until smooth and elastic.
5. Wrap the dough in plastic wrap and let it rest for at least 30 minutes.
6. Roll out the dough to your desired thickness and cut it into desired shapes using a pasta machine or hand.
7. Cook the pasta in boiling salted water for 2-3 minutes or until al dente. Serve with your favorite sauce and toppings.

Squid Ink Pasta Dough

Squid Ink Pasta Dough introduces a striking black color and a subtle salty flavor to your homemade pasta. Made with squid ink, this dough offers a unique and visually stunning addition to your pasta repertoire. Pair it with seafood or light cream-based sauces to complement its distinct taste.

Total Time Cooking: Approximately 1 hour

Ingredients:

- 2 cups all-purpose flour
- 1 tablespoon squid ink
- 2 large eggs
- 1/2 teaspoon salt

Directions:

1. combine all-purpose flour, squid ink, and salt in a mixing bowl.
2. Make a well in the center and add the eggs.
3. Gradually incorporate the flour into the eggs until a dough forms.
4. Knead the dough for 5-10 minutes until smooth and elastic.
5. Wrap the dough in plastic wrap and let it rest for at least 30 minutes.
6. Roll out the dough to your desired thickness and cut it into desired shapes using a pasta machine or hand.
7. Cook the pasta in boiling salted water for 2-3 minutes or until al dente. Serve with your favorite seafood sauce or toppings.

Chili Pepper Pasta Dough

Chili Pepper Pasta Dough adds a spicy kick to your homemade pasta. Made with chili pepper flakes or powder, this dough brings heat and flavor to your dishes. Pair it with a simple tomato sauce or a creamy garlic sauce to balance the spice.

Total Time Cooking: Approximately 1 hour

Ingredients:

- 2 cups all-purpose flour
- 1 tablespoon chili pepper flakes or powder
- 2 large eggs
- 1/2 teaspoon salt

Directions:

1. combine all-purpose flour, chili pepper flakes or powder, and salt in a mixing bowl.

2. Make a well in the center and add the eggs.

3. Gradually incorporate the flour into the eggs until a dough forms.

4. Knead the dough for 5-10 minutes until smooth and elastic.

5. Wrap the dough in plastic wrap and let it rest for at least 30 minutes.

6. Roll out the dough to your desired thickness and cut it into desired shapes using a pasta machine or hand.

7. Cook the pasta in boiling salted water for 2-3 minutes or until al dente. Serve with your preferred sauce or toppings.

Saffron Pasta Dough

Saffron Pasta Dough adds a luxurious golden color and a delicate floral flavor to your homemade pasta. Made with saffron threads infused in warm water, this dough is elegant and aromatic. Pair it with seafood or a creamy sauce for an indulgent dining experience.

Total Time Cooking: Approximately 1 hour

Ingredients:

- 2 cups all-purpose flour
- 1 tablespoon saffron threads
- 2 tablespoons warm water
- 2 large eggs
- 1/2 teaspoon salt

Directions:

1. In a small bowl, steep saffron threads in warm water for 10-15 minutes to release the color and flavor.

2. In a mixing bowl, combine all-purpose flour and salt.

3. Make a well in the center and add the saffron-infused water and eggs.

4. Gradually incorporate the flour into the wet ingredients until a dough forms.

5. Knead the dough for 5-10 minutes until smooth and elastic.

6. Wrap the dough in plastic wrap and let it rest for at least 30 minutes.

7. Roll out the dough to your desired thickness and cut it into desired shapes using a pasta machine or hand.

8.   Cook the pasta in boiling salted water for 2-3 minutes or until al dente. Serve with your preferred sauce or toppings.

Porcini Mushroom Pasta Dough

Porcini Mushroom Pasta Dough infuses your homemade pasta with dried porcini mushrooms' rich and earthy flavor. Ground porcini mushrooms are mixed into the dough, creating a unique and savory pasta. Pair it with a creamy mushroom sauce or a simple garlic and herb butter for a comforting meal.

Total Time Cooking: Approximately 1 hour

Ingredients:

- 2 cups all-purpose flour
- 1/4 cup dried porcini mushrooms, ground into powder
- 2 large eggs
- 1/2 teaspoon salt

Directions:

1. grind dried porcini mushrooms into a fine powder in a food processor.
2. combine all-purpose flour, ground porcini mushrooms, and salt in a mixing bowl.
3. Make a well in the center and add the eggs.
4. Gradually incorporate the flour into the eggs until a dough forms.
5. Knead the dough for 5-10 minutes until smooth and elastic.
6. Wrap the dough in plastic wrap and let it rest for at least 30 minutes.
7. Roll out the dough to your desired thickness and cut it into desired shapes using a pasta machine or hand.
8. Cook the pasta in boiling salted water for 2-3 minutes or until al dente. Serve with your favorite sauce and toppings.

Carrot Pasta Dough

Carrot Pasta Dough adds a subtle sweetness and a vibrant orange color to your homemade pasta. Made with pureed carrots, this dough is visually appealing and packed with nutrients. It's a great way to incorporate more vegetables into your meal while enjoying delicious pasta. Serve it with a creamy Alfredo sauce or a simple olive oil and garlic dressing for a delightful dish.

Total Time Cooking: Approximately 1 hour

Ingredients:

- 2 cups all-purpose flour
- 1/2 cup pureed carrots
- 2 large eggs
- 1/2 teaspoon salt

Directions:

1. combine all-purpose flour, pureed carrots, and salt in a mixing bowl.

2. Make a well in the center and add the eggs.

3. Gradually incorporate the flour into the eggs until a dough forms.

4. Knead the dough for 5-10 minutes until smooth and elastic.

5. Wrap the dough in plastic wrap and let it rest for at least 30 minutes.

6. Roll out the dough to your desired thickness and cut it into desired shapes using a pasta machine or hand.

7. Cook the pasta in boiling salted water for 2-3 minutes or until al dente. Serve with your favorite sauce and toppings.

Hibiscus Pasta Dough

Hibiscus Pasta Dough offers a beautiful pink color and a subtle floral flavor to your homemade pasta. Made with hibiscus tea or dried flowers, this dough is visually stunning and delicious. Pair it with a light lemon and herb sauce or a tangy tomato salsa for a refreshing and vibrant dish.

Total Time Cooking: Approximately 1 hour

Ingredients:

- 2 cups all-purpose flour
- 1/4 cup hibiscus tea or dried hibiscus flowers, steeped in hot water and pureed
- 2 large eggs
- 1/2 teaspoon salt

Directions:

1. combine all-purpose flour, hibiscus puree, and salt in a mixing bowl.
2. Make a well in the center and add the eggs.
3. Gradually incorporate the flour into the eggs until a dough forms.
4. Knead the dough for 5-10 minutes until smooth and elastic.
5. Wrap the dough in plastic wrap and let it rest for at least 30 minutes.
6. Roll out the dough to your desired thickness and cut it into desired shapes using a pasta machine or hand.
7. Cook the pasta in boiling salted water for 2-3 minutes or until al dente. Serve with your favorite sauce and toppings.

Beetroot Pasta Dough

Beetroot Pasta Dough adds a rich purple color and a sweet, earthy flavor to your homemade pasta. Made with pureed roasted beets, this dough is visually striking and delicious. Pair it with a creamy goat cheese sauce or a light balsamic vinaigrette for a delightful and nutritious meal.

Total Time Cooking: Approximately 1 hour

Ingredients:

- 2 cups all-purpose flour
- 1/2 cup pureed roasted beets
- 2 large eggs
- 1/2 teaspoon salt

Directions:

1. combine all-purpose flour, pureed beets, and salt in a mixing bowl.
2. Make a well in the center and add the eggs.
3. Gradually incorporate the flour into the eggs until a dough forms.
4. Knead the dough for 5-10 minutes until smooth and elastic.
5. Wrap the dough in plastic wrap and let it rest for at least 30 minutes.
6. Roll out the dough to your desired thickness and cut it into desired shapes using a pasta machine or hand.
7. Cook the pasta in boiling salted water for 2-3 minutes or until al dente. Serve with your favorite sauce and toppings.

Coconut Pasta Dough

Coconut Pasta Dough adds a tropical twist to your homemade pasta with coconut's subtle flavor and aroma. Made with coconut milk and shredded coconut, this dough offers a unique and indulgent dining experience. Pair it with a spicy Thai curry or a creamy coconut sauce for a delicious and satisfying meal.

Total Time Cooking: Approximately 1 hour

Ingredients:

- 2 cups all-purpose flour
- 1/2 cup coconut milk
- 1/4 cup shredded coconut
- 2 large eggs
- 1/2 teaspoon salt

Directions:

1. combine all-purpose flour, coconut milk, shredded coconut, and salt in a mixing bowl.

2. Make a well in the center and add the eggs.

3. Gradually incorporate the flour into the eggs until a dough forms.

4. Knead the dough for 5-10 minutes until smooth and elastic.

5. Wrap the dough in plastic wrap and let it rest for at least 30 minutes.

6. Roll out the dough to your desired thickness and cut it into desired shapes using a pasta machine or hand.

7. Cook the pasta in boiling salted water for 2-3 minutes or until al dente. Serve with your favorite sauce and toppings.

Lavender Pasta Dough

Lavender Pasta Dough brings a delicate floral aroma and subtle flavor to your homemade pasta. Made with culinary-grade dried lavender buds, this dough offers a fragrant and elegant twist on traditional pasta. Pair it with a light lemon butter sauce or a creamy goat cheese sauce for a delightful and sophisticated dish.

Total Time Cooking: Approximately 1 hour

Ingredients:

- 2 cups all-purpose flour
- 1 tablespoon culinary-grade dried lavender buds, finely ground
- 2 large eggs
- 1/2 teaspoon salt

Directions:

1. combine all-purpose flour, ground-dried lavender buds, and salt in a mixing bowl.

2. Make a well in the center and add the eggs.

3. Gradually incorporate the flour into the eggs until a dough forms.

4. Knead the dough for 5-10 minutes until smooth and elastic.

5. Wrap the dough in plastic wrap and let it rest for at least 30 minutes.

6. Roll out the dough to your desired thickness and cut it into desired shapes using a pasta machine or hand.

7. Cook the pasta in boiling salted water for 2-3 minutes or until al dente. Serve with your preferred sauce or toppings.

Butternut Squash Pasta Dough

Butternut Squash Pasta Dough adds a subtle sweetness and vibrant orange hue to your homemade pasta. This dough is made with pureed roasted butternut squash and offers a nutritious and flavorful twist. Pair it with a sage brown butter sauce or a creamy garlic and Parmesan sauce for a comforting and satisfying meal.

Total Time Cooking: Approximately 1 hour

Ingredients:

- 2 cups all-purpose flour
- 1/2 cup pureed roasted butternut squash
- 2 large eggs
- 1/2 teaspoon salt

Directions:

1. combine all-purpose flour, pureed roasted butternut squash, and salt in a mixing bowl.

2. Make a well in the center and add the eggs.

3. Gradually incorporate the flour into the eggs until a dough forms.

4. Knead the dough for 5-10 minutes until smooth and elastic.

5. Wrap the dough in plastic wrap and let it rest for at least 30 minutes.

6. Roll out the dough to your desired thickness and cut it into desired shapes using a pasta machine or hand.

7. Cook the pasta in boiling salted water for 2-3 minutes or until al dente. Serve with your preferred sauce or toppings.

Ginger Turmeric Pasta Dough

Ginger Turmeric Pasta Dough infuses your homemade pasta with warm and aromatic flavors. This dough is made with ground ginger and turmeric and offers a unique and vibrant twist. Pair it with a spicy peanut sauce or a coconut curry for a flavorful and exotic dish.

Total Time Cooking: Approximately 1 hour

Ingredients:

- 2 cups all-purpose flour
- 1 tablespoon ground ginger
- 1 tablespoon ground turmeric
- 2 large eggs
- 1/2 teaspoon salt

Directions:

1. combine all-purpose flour, ginger, turmeric, and salt in a mixing bowl.

2. Make a well in the center and add the eggs.

3. Gradually incorporate the flour into the eggs until a dough forms.

4. Knead the dough for 5-10 minutes until smooth and elastic.

5. Wrap the dough in plastic wrap and let it rest for at least 30 minutes.

6. Roll out the dough to your desired thickness and cut it into desired shapes using a pasta machine or hand.

7. Cook the pasta in boiling salted water for 2-3 minutes or until al dente. Serve with your preferred sauce or toppings.

Lemon Basil Pasta Dough

Lemon Basil Pasta Dough adds a refreshing citrusy flavor and aromatic basil notes to your homemade pasta. Made with fresh lemon zest and basil leaves, this dough is bright and flavorful. Pair it with a simple marinara sauce or a zesty lemon garlic sauce for a light and delicious meal.

Total Time Cooking: Approximately 1 hour

Ingredients:

- 2 cups all-purpose flour
- Zest of 2 lemons
- 1/4 cup fresh basil leaves, finely chopped
- 2 large eggs
- 1/2 teaspoon salt

Directions:

1. combine all-purpose flour, lemon zest, chopped basil leaves, and salt in a mixing bowl.
2. Make a well in the center and add the eggs.
3. Gradually incorporate the flour into the eggs until a dough forms.
4. Knead the dough for 5-10 minutes until smooth and elastic.
5. Wrap the dough in plastic wrap and let it rest for at least 30 minutes.
6. Roll out the dough to your desired thickness and cut it into desired shapes using a pasta machine or hand.
7. Cook the pasta in boiling salted water for 2-3 minutes or until al dente. Serve with your preferred sauce or toppings.

Whole Wheat Lasagna Dough

This whole wheat lasagna dough recipe adds a nutty flavor and extra nutritional value to your lasagna while maintaining a tender texture.

TOTAL TIME COOKING: Approximately 1 hour

Ingredients:

- 1 1/2 cups whole wheat flour
- 1/2 cup all-purpose flour
- 2 large eggs
- Pinch of salt

Directions:

1. Follow the same instructions as the classic lasagna dough recipe, but use a mixture of whole wheat and all-purpose flour.

2. Knead the dough until smooth and elastic, then let it rest and roll out as directed.

Spinach Lasagna Dough

This spinach lasagna dough recipe adds vibrant color and a subtle earthy flavor to your lasagna, making it both visually appealing and delicious.

TOTAL TIME COOKING: Approximately 1 hour

Ingredients:

- 2 cups all-purpose flour
- 2 large eggs
- 1/2 cup cooked and pureed spinach
- Pinch of salt

Directions:

1. Cook fresh spinach until wilted, then drain and puree it in a blender or food processor.

2. Follow the same instructions as the classic lasagna dough recipe, but incorporate the pureed spinach into the egg mixture.

3. Knead the dough until smooth and elastic, then let it rest and roll out as directed.

Herb Lasagna Dough

This herb lasagna dough recipe infuses your pasta with the flavors of fresh herbs, adding a fragrant and aromatic element to your lasagna.

TOTAL TIME COOKING: Approximately 1 hour

Ingredients:

- 2 cups all-purpose flour
- 2 large eggs
- 2 tablespoons finely chopped fresh herbs (such as parsley, basil, or thyme)
- Pinch of salt

Directions:

1. Finely chop your choice of fresh herbs.
2. Follow the same instructions as the classic lasagna dough recipe, but incorporate the chopped herbs into the egg mixture.
3. Knead the dough until smooth and elastic, then let it rest and roll out as directed.

Almond Flour Lasagna Dough

This almond flour lasagna dough recipe is perfect for those looking for a lower-carb alternative to traditional pasta. With a nutty flavor and slightly chewy texture, this dough pairs well with a variety of sauces and fillings.

TOTAL TIME COOKING: Approximately 1 hour

Ingredients:

- 2 cups almond flour
- 2 large eggs
- Pinch of salt

Directions:

1. In a mixing bowl, combine the almond flour and salt.

2. Create a well in the center of the flour mixture and crack the eggs into it.

3. Using a fork, gradually mix the eggs into the almond flour until a dough forms.

4. Knead the dough for about 5-7 minutes until it becomes smooth and elastic.

5. Wrap the dough in plastic wrap and let it rest at room temperature for 30 minutes.

6. Roll out the dough into thin sheets using a pasta roller or a rolling pin.

7. Cut the sheets into lasagna noodles of desired size and use them to assemble your lasagna.

Brown Rice Lasagna Dough

This brown rice lasagna dough recipe offers a wholesome and nutritious alternative to traditional pasta. Made with brown rice flour, this dough has a slightly nutty flavor and pairs well with a variety of sauces and fillings.

TOTAL TIME COOKING: Approximately 1 hour

Ingredients:

- 2 cups brown rice flour
- 2 large eggs
- Pinch of salt

Directions:

1. In a mixing bowl, combine the brown rice flour and salt.

2. Create a well in the center of the flour mixture and crack the eggs into it.

3. Using a fork, gradually mix the eggs into the brown rice flour until a dough forms.

4. Knead the dough for about 5-7 minutes until it becomes smooth and elastic.

5. Wrap the dough in plastic wrap and let it rest at room temperature for 30 minutes.

6. Roll out the dough into thin sheets using a pasta roller or a rolling pin.

7. Cut the sheets into lasagna noodles of desired size and use them to assemble your lasagna.

Quinoa Flour Lasagna Dough

This quinoa flour lasagna dough recipe offers a gluten-free and protein-rich option for making homemade pasta. With a delicate flavor and tender texture, this dough is perfect for creating delicious lasagna dishes.

TOTAL TIME COOKING: Approximately 1 hour

Ingredients:

- 2 cups quinoa flour
- 2 large eggs
- Pinch of salt

Directions:

1. In a mixing bowl, combine the quinoa flour and salt.
2. Create a well in the center of the flour mixture and crack the eggs into it.
3. Using a fork, gradually mix the eggs into the quinoa flour until a dough forms.
4. Knead the dough for about 5-7 minutes until it becomes smooth and elastic.
5. Wrap the dough in plastic wrap and let it rest at room temperature for 30 minutes.
6. Roll out the dough into thin sheets using a pasta roller or a rolling pin.
7. Cut the sheets into lasagna noodles of desired size and use them to assemble your lasagna.

Tapioca Flour Lasagna Dough

This tapioca flour lasagna dough recipe produces a soft and pliable pasta perfect for layering in lasagna dishes. Tapioca flour adds a unique texture to the dough, making it both tender and chewy.

TOTAL TIME COOKING: Approximately 1 hour

Ingredients:

- 2 cups tapioca flour
- 2 large eggs
- Pinch of salt

Directions:

1. In a mixing bowl, combine the tapioca flour and salt.

2. Create a well in the center of the flour mixture and crack the eggs into it.

3. Using a fork, gradually mix the eggs into the tapioca flour until a dough forms.

4. Knead the dough for about 5-7 minutes until it becomes smooth and elastic.

5. Wrap the dough in plastic wrap and let it rest at room temperature for 30 minutes.

6. Roll out the dough into thin sheets using a pasta roller or a rolling pin.

7. Cut the sheets into lasagna noodles of desired size and use them to assemble your lasagna.

Pasta Sause

Classic Marinara Sauce

This classic marinara sauce is a simple and versatile option for pasta lovers. Made with tomatoes, garlic, onions, and herbs, this sauce quickly prepares and bursts with flavor. Use it as a base for your favorite pasta dishes or a dipping sauce for garlic bread.

Total Time Cooking: Approximately 30 minutes

Ingredients:

- 2 tablespoons olive oil
- 3 cloves garlic, minced
- 1 onion, diced
- 1 can (28 oz) crushed tomatoes
- 1 teaspoon dried oregano
- 1 teaspoon dried basil
- Salt and pepper to taste
- Fresh basil leaves for garnish (optional)

Directions:

1. Heat olive oil in a saucepan over medium heat. Add minced garlic, diced onion, and sauté until softened and fragrant, about 5 minutes.

2. Stir in crushed tomatoes, dried oregano, and dried basil. Season with salt and pepper to taste.

3. Bring the sauce to a simmer, then reduce the heat to low. Let it simmer for 15-20 minutes, stirring occasionally, until the flavors have melded together and the sauce has thickened.

4. Taste and adjust seasoning if necessary. Serve hot over, cooked pasta, garnished with fresh basil leaves if desired.

Creamy Alfredo Sauce

Creamy Alfredo sauce is a decadent and indulgent option for pasta nights. This sauce is rich, velvety, and irresistibly delicious, made with butter, cream, garlic, and Parmesan cheese. Pair it with fettuccine or penne for a classic pasta dish that's sure to satisfy.

Total Time Cooking: Approximately 20 minutes

Ingredients:

- 1/2 cup unsalted butter
- 3 cloves garlic, minced
- 1 cup heavy cream
- 1 cup grated Parmesan cheese
- Salt and pepper to taste
- Fresh parsley for garnish (optional)

Directions:

1. In a saucepan, melt butter over medium heat. Add minced garlic and sauté until fragrant, about 1 minute.

2. Stir in heavy cream and bring to a simmer. Let it cook for 5-7 minutes, stirring occasionally, until slightly thickened.

3. Gradually add grated Parmesan cheese to the sauce, stirring continuously until the cheese is melted and smooth.

4. Season with salt and pepper to taste.

5. Remove the sauce from heat and toss with cooked pasta until well coated.

6. Serve hot, garnished with fresh parsley if desired.

Spicy Arrabbiata Sauce

The spicy arrabbiata sauce packs a punch with its bold flavors and fiery kick. Made with tomatoes, red pepper flakes, garlic, and olive oil, this sauce is perfect for those who enjoy a bit of heat in their pasta dishes. Pair it with penne or spaghetti for a satisfying meal with a spicy twist.

Total Time Cooking: Approximately 30 minutes

Ingredients:

- 2 tablespoons olive oil
- 3 cloves garlic, minced
- 1 can (28 oz) crushed tomatoes
- 1 teaspoon red pepper flakes (adjust to taste)
- 1 teaspoon dried oregano
- Salt to taste
- Fresh basil leaves for garnish (optional)

Directions:

1. Heat olive oil in a saucepan over medium heat. Add minced garlic and sauté until fragrant, about 1 minute.

2. Stir in crushed tomatoes, red pepper flakes, and dried oregano. Season with salt to taste.

3. Bring the sauce to a simmer, then reduce the heat to low. Let it simmer for 20-25 minutes, stirring occasionally, until the flavors have melded together and the sauce has thickened.

4. Taste and adjust seasoning if necessary. Serve hot over, cooked pasta, garnished with fresh basil leaves if desired.

Pesto Sauce

Pesto sauce offers fresh flavors and vibrant green color to your pasta dishes. Made with fresh basil, pine nuts, garlic, Parmesan cheese, and olive oil, this sauce is quick to prepare and incredibly delicious. Toss it with your favorite pasta for a taste of Italy in every bite.

Total Time Cooking: Approximately 10 minutes

Ingredients:

- 2 cups fresh basil leaves
- 1/4 cup pine nuts
- 2 cloves garlic
- 1/2 cup grated Parmesan cheese
- 1/2 cup extra virgin olive oil
- Salt and pepper to taste

Directions:

1. combine fresh basil leaves, pine nuts, garlic, and grated Parmesan cheese in a food processor. Pulse until finely chopped.

2. With the food processor running, slowly drizzle in the olive oil until the pesto reaches your desired consistency. Season with salt and pepper to taste.

3. Toss the pesto with cooked pasta until well-coated. Serve hot.

Roasted Red Pepper Sauce

Roasted red pepper sauce offers your pasta dishes a sweet and smoky flavor. This sauce is creamy, flavorful, and easy to make, made with roasted red peppers, garlic, onions, and a touch of cream. Pair it with rigatoni or farfalle for a delicious meal that's sure to impress.

Total Time Cooking: Approximately 40 minutes

Ingredients:

- 2 large red bell peppers
- 2 tablespoons olive oil
- 3 cloves garlic, minced
- 1 onion, diced
- 1/2 cup heavy cream
- Salt and pepper to taste
- Fresh basil leaves for garnish (optional)

Directions:

1. Preheat the oven to 400°F (200°C). Line a baking sheet with parchment paper.

2. Cut the red bell peppers in half lengthwise and remove the seeds and membranes. Place them cut-side down on the prepared baking sheet.

3. Roast the peppers in the oven for 25-30 minutes or until the skins are charred and blistered.

4. Remove the peppers from the oven and let them cool slightly. Peel off the skins and discard.

5. In a saucepan, heat olive oil over medium heat. Add minced garlic, diced onion, and sauté until softened and fragrant, about 5 minutes.

6. Add roasted red peppers to the saucepan and cook for 2-3 minutes.

7. Transfer the mixture to a blender and puree until smooth.

8. Return the pureed sauce to the saucepan. Stir in heavy cream and bring to a simmer. Let it cook for 5-7 minutes, stirring occasionally, until slightly thickened.

9. Season with salt and pepper to taste. Serve hot over, cooked pasta, garnished with fresh basil leaves if desired.

Lemon Garlic Butter Sauce

Lemon garlic butter sauce is a light and refreshing option for pasta lovers. Made with butter, garlic, lemon juice, and fresh parsley, this sauce bursts with bright flavors and pairs well with various pasta shapes. It's perfect for a quick weeknight dinner or a cozy Sunday brunch.

Total Time Cooking: Approximately 15 minutes

Ingredients:

- 4 tablespoons unsalted butter
- 3 cloves garlic, minced
- Zest and juice of 1 lemon
- 1/4 cup chopped fresh parsley
- Salt and pepper to taste
- Grated Parmesan cheese for garnish (optional)

Directions:

1. In a skillet, melt butter over medium heat. Add minced garlic and cook until fragrant, about 1 minute.

2. Stir in lemon zest and lemon juice. Season with salt and pepper to taste.

3. Add chopped parsley to the skillet and toss to combine.

4. Toss the sauce with cooked pasta until well-coated. Serve hot, garnished with grated Parmesan cheese if desired.

Mushroom Cream Sauce

Mushroom cream sauce is a rich and indulgent option for pasta nights. This sauce is velvety smooth and packed with savory flavors and made with sautéed mushrooms, garlic, onions, and cream. Pair it with fettuccine or gnocchi for a comforting and satisfying meal.

Total Time Cooking: Approximately 25 minutes

Ingredients:

- 2 tablespoons olive oil
- 8 ounces mushrooms, sliced
- 3 cloves garlic, minced
- 1/2 onion, diced
- 1 cup heavy cream
- 1/4 cup grated Parmesan cheese
- Salt and pepper to taste
- Fresh parsley for garnish (optional)

Directions:

1. Heat olive oil in a skillet over medium heat. Add sliced mushrooms and cook until golden brown, about 5-7 minutes.

2. Add minced garlic and diced onion to the skillet. Sauté until softened and fragrant, about 3-4 minutes.

3. Pour in heavy cream and bring to a simmer. Let it cook for 5-7 minutes, stirring occasionally, until slightly thickened.

4. Stir in grated Parmesan cheese until melted and smooth. Season with salt and pepper to taste.

5. Toss the sauce with cooked pasta until well-coated. Serve hot, garnished with fresh parsley if desired.

Spinach and Tomato Sauce

Spinach and tomato sauce is a vibrant and nutritious option for pasta dishes. Made with fresh spinach, cherry tomatoes, garlic, and herbs, this sauce is packed with vitamins and antioxidants. Pair it with spaghetti or penne for a wholesome and delicious meal.

Total Time Cooking: Approximately 20 minutes

Ingredients:

- 2 tablespoons olive oil
- 3 cloves garlic, minced
- 2 cups cherry tomatoes, halved
- 4 cups fresh spinach leaves
- 1 teaspoon dried Italian herbs (such as basil, oregano, and thyme)
- Salt and pepper to taste
- Grated Parmesan cheese for garnish (optional)

Directions:

1. Heat olive oil in a skillet over medium heat. Add minced garlic and cook until fragrant, about 1 minute.

2. Add cherry tomatoes to the skillet and cook until softened, about 5 minutes.

3. Stir in fresh spinach leaves and dried Italian herbs. Cook until the spinach wilts, about 2-3 minutes.

4. Season with salt and pepper to taste.

5. Toss the sauce with cooked pasta until well combined. Serve hot, garnished with grated Parmesan cheese if desired.

Roasted Vegetable Sauce

Roasted vegetable sauce is a hearty and flavorful option for pasta lovers. Made with a variety of roasted vegetables, such as bell peppers, zucchini, and eggplant, this sauce is rich, savory, and packed with natural sweetness. Pair it with rigatoni or fusilli for a satisfying and nutritious meal.

Total Time Cooking: Approximately 40 minutes

Ingredients:

- 1 red bell pepper, diced
- 1 yellow bell pepper, diced
- 1 zucchini, diced
- 1 eggplant, diced
- 2 tablespoons olive oil
- 3 cloves garlic, minced
- 1 can (14 oz) diced tomatoes
- 1 teaspoon dried Italian herbs (such as basil, oregano, and thyme)
- Salt and pepper to taste
- Fresh basil leaves for garnish (optional)

Directions:

1. Preheat the oven to 400°F (200°C). Line a baking sheet with parchment paper.

2. In a large bowl, toss diced bell peppers, zucchini, and eggplant with olive oil until evenly coated. Spread the vegetables in a single layer on the prepared baking sheet.

3. Roast the vegetables in the oven for 25-30 minutes or until tender and caramelized.

4. In a skillet, heat olive oil over medium heat. Add minced garlic and cook until fragrant, about 1 minute.

5. Stir in diced tomatoes and dried Italian herbs. Cook for 5-7 minutes, stirring occasionally, until the sauce thickens slightly.

6. Add roasted vegetables to the skillet and toss to combine. Season with salt and pepper to taste.

7. Toss the sauce with cooked pasta until well-coated. Serve hot, garnished with fresh basil leaves if desired.

Garlic Mushroom Marinara Sauce

This garlic mushroom marinara sauce is packed with savory flavors and hearty textures, making it a satisfying option for vegan pasta dishes. Sautéed mushrooms and garlic are simmered in a rich tomato sauce with herbs, creating a comforting and delicious meal in no time.

Total Time Cooking: Approximately 30 minutes

Ingredients:

- 2 tablespoons olive oil
- 8 ounces mushrooms, sliced
- 4 cloves garlic, minced
- 1 can (28 oz) crushed tomatoes
- 1 teaspoon dried oregano
- 1 teaspoon dried basil
- Salt and pepper to taste
- Fresh basil leaves for garnish (optional)

Directions:

1. Heat olive oil in a skillet over medium heat. Add sliced mushrooms and cook until golden brown, about 5-7 minutes.

2. Add minced garlic to the skillet and sauté until fragrant, about 1 minute.

3. Stir in crushed tomatoes, dried oregano, and dried basil. Season with salt and pepper to taste.

4. Bring the sauce to a simmer, then reduce the heat to low. Let it simmer for 15-20 minutes, stirring occasionally.

5. Taste and adjust seasoning if necessary. Serve hot over, cooked pasta, garnished with fresh basil leaves if desired.

Lemon Ricotta Pasta Sauce

This Lemon Ricotta Pasta Sauce is a delightful twist on traditional pasta sauces. Its creamy texture and bright citrus flavor make it a refreshing choice for any pasta dish. It's perfect for a quick and flavorful meal with a total cooking time of just 15 minutes.

TOTAL TIME COOKING: Approximately 15 minutes

Ingredients:

- 1 cup ricotta cheese
- Zest and juice of 1 lemon
- 2 tablespoons olive oil
- 2 cloves garlic, minced
- 1/4 cup chopped fresh basil
- Salt and pepper to taste
- Cooked pasta of your choice

Directions:

1. combine ricotta cheese, lemon zest, and lemon juice in a bowl. Mix until well combined.

2. Heat olive oil in a skillet over medium heat. Add minced garlic and sauté until fragrant.

3. Add the ricotta mixture to the skillet and stir until heated.

4. Stir in chopped fresh basil and season with salt and pepper to taste.

5. Toss the sauce with cooked pasta until well-coated. Serve hot.

Coconut Curry Pasta Sauce

This Coconut Curry Pasta Sauce offers a fusion of Asian and Italian flavors, creating a unique and aromatic sauce that will tantalize your taste buds. With a total cooking time of 30 minutes, it's perfect for a flavorful and satisfying dinner.

TOTAL TIME COOKING: Approximately 30 minutes

Ingredients:

- 1 tablespoon coconut oil
- 1 onion, diced
- 2 cloves garlic, minced
- 1 tablespoon curry powder
- 1 can (14 oz) coconut milk
- 1 cup vegetable broth
- 2 tablespoons soy sauce
- 1 tablespoon maple syrup
- Salt and pepper to taste
- Cooked pasta of your choice
- Chopped cilantro for garnish (optional)

Directions:

1. Heat coconut oil in a skillet over medium heat. Add diced onion and sauté until translucent.

2. Add minced garlic and curry powder to the skillet and cook until fragrant.

3. Pour coconut milk, vegetable broth, soy sauce, and maple syrup. Stir until well combined.

4. Simmer the sauce for 15-20 minutes or until it thickens slightly. Season with salt and pepper to taste.

5. Toss the sauce with cooked pasta until well-coated. Serve hot, garnished with chopped cilantro if desired.

Sun-Dried Tomato Pesto Pasta Sauce

This Sun-Dried Tomato Pesto Pasta Sauce is a flavorful and vibrant option for pasta lovers. Combining sun-dried tomatoes, basil, garlic, and pine nuts creates a rich and aromatic sauce that will elevate any pasta dish. With a total cooking time of 20 minutes, it's perfect for a quick and delicious meal.

TOTAL TIME COOKING: Approximately 20 minutes

Ingredients:

- 1 cup sun-dried tomatoes (packed in oil), drained
- 2 cloves garlic
- 1/4 cup pine nuts
- 1/4 cup grated Parmesan cheese (optional for non-vegan)
- 1/4 cup olive oil
- Salt and pepper to taste
- Cooked pasta of your choice
- Fresh basil leaves for garnish

Directions:

1. In a food processor, combine sun-dried tomatoes, garlic, pine nuts, and grated Parmesan cheese (if using). Pulse until finely chopped.

2. With the food processor running, slowly drizzle in olive oil until the mixture forms a smooth paste.

3. Season the pesto with salt and pepper to taste.

4. Toss the pesto with cooked pasta until well-coated. Serve hot, garnished with fresh basil leaves.

Ginger Miso Pasta Sauce

This Ginger Miso Pasta Sauce is a unique and savory option that combines the flavors of ginger, miso, and sesame for a delicious umami-packed sauce. With a total cooking time of 25 minutes, it's perfect for a quick and flavorful meal that will satisfy you.

TOTAL TIME COOKING: Approximately 25 minutes

Ingredients:

- 2 tablespoons sesame oil
- 2 cloves garlic, minced
- 1 tablespoon grated ginger
- 3 tablespoons white miso paste
- 1 cup vegetable broth
- 2 tablespoons soy sauce
- 1 tablespoon maple syrup
- 2 teaspoons cornstarch mixed with 2 tablespoons water (optional for thickening)
- Cooked pasta of your choice
- Sliced green onions for garnish (optional)
- Sesame seeds for garnish (optional)

Directions:

1. Heat sesame oil in a skillet over medium heat. Add minced garlic and grated ginger, and sauté until fragrant.
2. Stir in white miso paste, vegetable broth, soy sauce, and maple syrup. Bring the mixture to a simmer.

3.	If desired, add the cornstarch mixture to the skillet to thicken the sauce. Stir until the sauce thickens slightly.

4.	Toss the sauce with cooked pasta until well-coated. Serve hot, garnished with sliced green onions and sesame seeds if desired.

Creamy Walnut Sage Pasta Sauce

This Creamy Walnut Sage Pasta Sauce offers a unique and nutty flavor profile that pairs beautifully with pasta. Combining toasted walnuts, fresh sage, and creamy coconut milk creates a decadent and flavorful sauce to impress your guests. With a total cooking time of 20 minutes, it's perfect for a quick and elegant meal.

TOTAL TIME COOKING: Approximately 20 minutes

Ingredients:

- 1 cup walnuts
- 2 tablespoons olive oil
- 2 cloves garlic, minced
- 1/4 cup chopped fresh sage leaves
- 1 can (14 oz) coconut milk
- Salt and pepper to taste
- Cooked pasta of your choice
- Grated vegan Parmesan cheese for garnish (optional)

Directions:

1. In a dry skillet, toast walnuts over medium heat until fragrant and lightly browned. Remove from the skillet and let them cool.

2. In the same skillet, heat olive oil over medium heat. Add minced garlic and chopped fresh sage leaves, and sauté until fragrant.

3. Transfer the toasted walnuts to a food processor and pulse until finely chopped.

4. Add the chopped walnuts to the skillet and stir to combine.

5. Pour coconut milk and simmer the sauce for 5-7 minutes or until it thickens slightly—season with salt and pepper to taste.

6. Toss the sauce with cooked pasta until well-coated. Serve hot, garnished with grated vegan Parmesan cheese if desired.

Thai Peanut Sauce

Thai peanut sauce is a creamy and flavorful sauce that pairs perfectly with pasta for a delicious fusion dish. This sauce, made with peanut butter, coconut milk, soy sauce, lime juice, and Thai spices, adds a rich and savory flavor to any pasta dish.

TOTAL TIME COOKING: Approximately 10 minutes

Ingredients:

- 1/2 cup creamy peanut butter
- 1/2 cup coconut milk
- 2 tablespoons soy sauce or tamari
- 2 tablespoons lime juice
- 1 tablespoon maple syrup or brown sugar
- 1 clove garlic, minced
- 1 teaspoon grated ginger
- 1/2 teaspoon red pepper flakes (adjust to taste)
- Salt, to taste
- Water (as needed to thin out the sauce)

Directions:

1. In a small saucepan, combine the peanut butter, coconut milk, soy sauce, lime juice, maple syrup or brown sugar, minced garlic, grated ginger, and red pepper flakes.

2. Cook over low heat, stirring constantly, until the peanut butter is melted and the sauce is smooth and creamy. If the sauce is too thick, add water a tablespoon until it reaches your desired consistency.

3. Taste and adjust the seasoning with salt and red pepper flakes if desired.

4. Remove from heat and serve immediately over cooked pasta. Garnish with chopped peanuts, cilantro, and lime wedges if desired.

Thai Basil Pesto

Thai basil pesto is a fragrant and vibrant sauce that adds flavor to pasta dishes. This pesto is a delicious twist on the classic Italian sauce and is made with fresh Thai basil, garlic, peanuts, lime zest, and olive oil.

TOTAL TIME COOKING: Approximately 15 minutes

Ingredients:

- 2 cups fresh Thai basil leaves, packed
- 1/2 cup roasted peanuts
- 2 cloves garlic
- Zest and juice of 1 lime
- 1/4 cup olive oil
- Salt and pepper, to taste
- Red pepper flakes (optional, for added heat)

Directions:

1. combine the Thai basil leaves, roasted peanuts, garlic cloves, lime zest, and lime juice in a food processor.

2. Pulse until the ingredients are finely chopped.

3. With the food processor running, slowly drizzle in the olive oil until the pesto reaches your desired consistency.

4. Season with salt, pepper, and red pepper flakes to taste.

5. Serve the Thai basil pesto over cooked pasta and toss to coat. Garnish with additional fresh Thai basil leaves and roasted peanuts if desired.

Thai Green Curry Sauce

Thai green curry sauce is a creamy and aromatic sauce that adds flavor to pasta dishes. This sauce is perfect for a quick and easy weeknight meal and is made with coconut milk, green curry paste, lime juice, and Thai spices.

TOTAL TIME COOKING: Approximately 15 minutes

Ingredients:

- 1 can (13.5 oz) coconut milk
- 2-3 tablespoons green curry paste
- 1 tablespoon soy sauce or tamari
- 1 tablespoon lime juice
- 1 teaspoon maple syrup or brown sugar
- 1 clove garlic, minced
- 1 teaspoon grated ginger
- Salt, to taste
- Fresh cilantro for garnish

Directions:

1. In a saucepan, combine the coconut milk, green curry paste, soy sauce or tamari, lime juice, maple syrup or brown sugar, minced garlic, and grated ginger.

2. Cook over medium heat, stirring occasionally, until the sauce is heated through and slightly thickened.

3. Taste and adjust the seasoning with salt as needed.

4. Remove heat and serve the Thai green curry sauce over cooked pasta. Garnish with fresh cilantro before serving.

Thai Sweet Chili Sauce

Thai sweet chili sauce is a versatile and flavorful sauce that adds a touch of sweetness and heat to pasta dishes. Made with chili peppers, garlic, vinegar, and sugar, this sauce is perfect for drizzling over pasta or as a dipping sauce for spring rolls or dumplings.

TOTAL TIME COOKING: Approximately 15 minutes

Ingredients:

- 1/2 cup water
- 1/2 cup rice vinegar
- 1/2 cup granulated sugar
- 2 cloves garlic, minced
- 2-3 red chili peppers, thinly sliced
- 1 tablespoon cornstarch
- 2 tablespoons water

Directions:

1. combine the water, rice vinegar, sugar, minced garlic, and sliced chili peppers in a saucepan.

2. Bring the mixture to a simmer over medium heat, stirring occasionally, until the sugar dissolves.

3. whisk together the cornstarch and water in a small bowl to make a slurry.

4. Stir the cornstarch slurry into the saucepan and continue to simmer, stirring constantly, until the sauce has thickened.

5. Remove from heat and let the sauce cool slightly before serving.

6. Serve the Thai sweet chili sauce over cooked pasta or use it as a dipping sauce for spring rolls or dumplings. Enjoy the sweet and spicy flavors!

Vegetarian Carbonara Sauce

This vegetarian version of Carbonara sauce replaces the traditional pancetta or bacon with sautéed mushrooms for a flavorful and satisfying dish. This sauce, made with eggs, Parmesan cheese, mushrooms, garlic, and black pepper, is perfect for vegetarians and meat lovers.

TOTAL TIME COOKING: Approximately 25 minutes

Ingredients:

- 12 oz (340g) spaghetti or pasta of your choice
- 4 large eggs
- 1 cup grated Parmesan cheese
- 8 oz (225g) mushrooms, sliced
- 2 cloves garlic, minced
- 2 tablespoons olive oil
- Salt and black pepper, to taste
- Fresh parsley, chopped (for garnish, optional)

Directions:

1. Cook the spaghetti according to the package instructions until al dente. Reserve 1 cup of pasta water, drain the pasta and set aside.

2. In a mixing bowl, whisk the eggs, grated Parmesan cheese, salt, and black pepper until well combined. Set aside.

3. In a large skillet, heat olive oil over medium heat. Add the sliced mushrooms and cook until they release moisture and become golden brown, about 8-10 minutes. Add minced garlic and cook for an additional 1-2 minutes until fragrant.

4. Reduce the heat to low and add the cooked pasta to the skillet with the mushrooms. Toss to combine.

5. Remove the skillet from the heat and quickly pour the egg and cheese mixture over the pasta, stirring continuously until the eggs thicken and coat the pasta. If the sauce seems too thick, add a splash of reserved pasta water to loosen it.

6. Serve the Vegetarian Carbonara pasta immediately, garnished with chopped fresh parsley if desired. Enjoy this delicious meat-free version of a classic Italian dish!

Printed in Dunstable, United Kingdom